THE STARS

AUTHOR: Clint Twist
ILLUSTRATOR: Kuo Kang Chen
ART EDITOR: Duncan Brown
EDITOR: Elise See Tai
AMERICAN EDITOR: Nathan Hemmelgarn
ART DIRECTOR: Miranda Kennedy
EDITORIAL MANAGER: Ruth Hooper
PRODUCTION DIRECTOR: Clive Sparling

Created and produced by Andromeda Children's Books
An imprint of Pinwheel Ltd
Winchester House
259–269 Old Marylebone Road
London NW1 5XJ, UK

This edition published in 2006 by School Specialty Publishing, a member of the
School Specialty Family.

Library of Congress Cataloging-in-Publication Data is on file with the publisher.

Send all inquiries to: School Specialty Publishing
8720 Orion Place, Columbus, OH 43240-2111

ISBN 0-7696-4492-9

1 2 3 4 5 6 7 8 9 10 PIN 10 09 08 07 06

Printed in China

CONTENTS

THE SUN

The Sun shines brightly in space. Heat and light from the Sun make Earth a good place to live. The Sun is a star—the nearest star to Earth. It is one of billions of stars in the universe. A star is a very large ball of gas. Heat and light are produced by nuclear energy at the center of the star. All stars have the same basic structure, but there are many differences in their size and appearance. The Sun is a fairly small star with a yellowish color. It is classified as a *yellow dwarf star*.

MYTHS AND LEGENDS

Ancient Greek astronomers believed that the Earth was at the center of the universe. They believed that a series of transparent crystal spheres surrounded the Earth and contained the Sun, Moon, planets, and stars. According to Greek astronomers, the seventh and outermost crystal sphere held the stars.

Star Shapes

People see recognizable shapes in natural features, the Man in the Moon, for example, and stars are no exception. By joining together the brighter stars with lines, ancient people were able to "see" a variety of shapes in the night sky. Such arrangements of stars are known as *constellations*. Some constellations and their stories have been passed down through the ages. Constellations are still used today as a way to map the night sky.

Centaurus (the Centaur)

According to ancient Greek legend, a centaur was half human and half horse. The Centaurus constellation takes the shape of a centaur. Proxima Centauri, the red dwarf, is situated near the star Alpha Centauri in the front hooves. The Crux (cross) constellation appears close to Centaurus.

Big Dipper

Ursa Major (the Great Bear)

Legend says that a beautiful Greek girl was changed into a bear by a jealous goddess. The seven stars that form Ursa Major's tail and part of the body make the constellation known as the the *Big Dipper*.

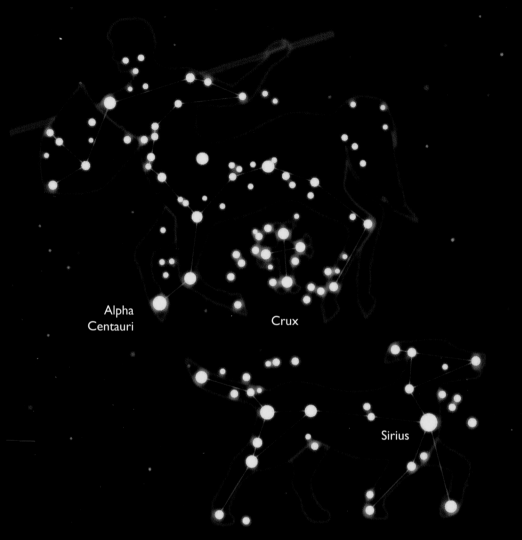

Alpha
Centauri

Crux

Sirius

Rigel

CANIS MAJOR (THE GREAT DOG)

Canis Major is one of two "star dogs" that appear close to Orion the Hunter. The very bright star Sirius, also known as the *Dog Star*, is located in the neck.

ORION (THE HUNTER)

Orion was a Greek hero remembered forever in the stars by the gods. The easiest stars to see are the three in Orion's belt. Rigel, a supergiant star, is located in the hunter's raised foot.

NIGHT SKIES

The night sky is never exactly the same two nights in a row. The stars appear to move very slowly across the sky. The many different constellations are seen according to an annual cycle. The apparent movement of the stars is a result of Earth's year-long orbit of the Sun. As Earth moves through space, the view of the stars changes accordingly.

STAR VIEWING

What is seen when looking up on a cloudless night depends on three things—the location on Earth in terms of longitude (position north or south of the Equator), the time of year, and the time of night. Longitude determines what part of the whole night sky can be seen. A person near the Equator will have a very different view than someone near the Poles. The time of year determines which constellations are visible from Earth according to the annual cycle. The time of night determines the exact position of the stars.

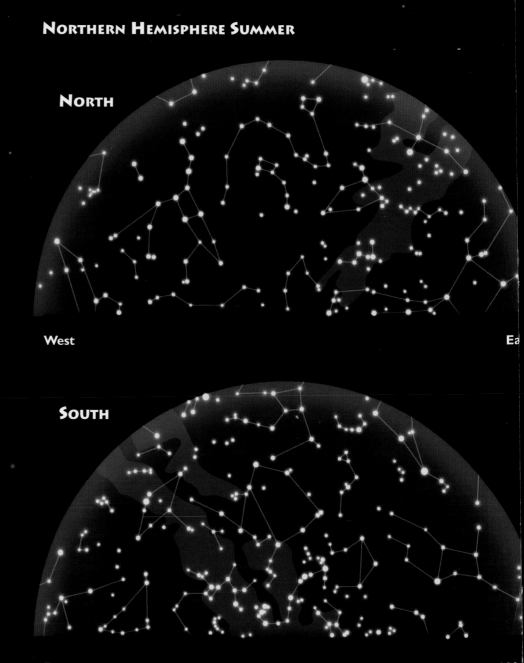

NORTHERN HEMISPHERE SUMMER

NORTH

West

Ea

SOUTH

East

We

LIFE CYCLE

A medium-sized star like the Sun has a life cycle
that lasts between eight and 12 billion years.

Deep inside a thick, dusty
nebula, a new star flares
into life. Material left
over from the star-making
process may form planets
that orbit the star, just
as Earth orbits the Sun.

For nearly all of its long, long
life, the star "burns" smoothly
and steadily with a bright yellow
light. At the core of the star, vast
amounts of energy are produced
by the element hydrogen being
converted into the element helium.

After billions of years, the star runs out of
hydrogen and begins converting helium instead.
The star gradually swells to more than 200 times
larger than it was and becomes a red giant with
a surface temperature of only about 5,400°F.

The star then shrinks suddenly, losing huge
quantities of mass as gases blow off into space.
What remains of the star becomes a small and
very hot, white dwarf at the center of an
expanding bubble of gases.